Editor
Eric Migliaccio

Managing Editor
Ina Massler Levin, M.A.

Editor-in-Chief
Sharon Coan, M.S. Ed.

Cover Artist
Barb Lorseyedi

Art Manager
Kevin Barnes

Art Director
CJae Froshay

Imaging
Rosa C. See

Product Manager
Phil Garcia

Publishers
Rachelle Cracchiolo, M.S. Ed.
Mary Dupuy Smith, M.S. Ed.

Building Better Literacy Skills: Syllables

Author

Gilly Czerwonka

Teacher Created Materials, Inc.
6421 Industry Way
Westminster, CA 92683
www.teachercreated.com

ISBN-0-7439-3239-0

©*2004 Teacher Created Materials, Inc.*

Made in U.S.A.

This edition is published with © Folens Limited

First published 2001 by Folens Limited.

United Kingdom: Folens Publishers, Apex Business Center, Boscombe Road, Dunstable, LU5 4RL.

Email: folens@folens.com

Gilly Czerwonka hereby asserts her moral right to be identified as the author of this work in accordance with the Copyright, Designs and Patents Act 1988.

Editor: Nicky Platt

Layout artist: Patricia Hollingsworth

Cover design: Martin Cross

Table of Contents—Book 2

Introduction to the Series

Building Basic Literacy Skills is a complete course for students in the early years of middle school. It has been divided into seven books for ease of use by teachers, tutors, and students. **This is *Book 2: Syllables*.** The following is a summary of each of the seven books in the series:

Book 1: Words
- covers the building and splitting of simple c-v-c (consonant-vowel-consonant) combinations and consonant blends

Book 2: Syllables
- covers breaking words into syllables and long vowel sounds

Book 3: Vowel Sounds
- covers the long vowel combinations and splitting syllables with long vowel sounds

Book 4: Word Beginnings and Endings
- deals with common prefixes and suffixes

Book 5: Complex Words
- deals with more complex multi-syllabic words and further common prefixes and suffixes

Book 6: Irregular Words
- deals with words that follow less common, or seemingly no, spelling patterns (often called "high frequency" vocabulary)

Book 7: Spelling
- comprises material for the checking and recording of progress in the spelling of words learned, through simple tests and activities

The units in the these books work well when taught in order. If determined appropriate by the teacher, however, the units are designed so that they can be used in any order.

- Many students enter the middle-school phase of school unable to take full control of their reading—and more particularly their spelling—from a lack of knowledge of how letters work within words. If this is uncorrected, the sheer volume of reading and writing demanded during the middle-school years may leave them at a severe disadvantage.

- For some of these students, their potential for understanding information is marred by an inability to work quickly and automatically to decode and encode words. The *Building Basic Literacy Skills* program is designed to help them.

Introduction to the Series *(cont.)*

- Set out in unit lessons, it is aimed as a "second chance" for students who require extra support in basic understanding of the phonics, word, and syllable knowledge needed for reading and spelling.

- The units are designed to be delivered through extra daily sessions which may be monitored by a teacher, support teacher, support assistant, or tutor.

- Each unit follows a similar pattern of delivery, enabling students to work with the minimum of tutor preparation and guidance.

- Optimum group size will be dependent on the rate and speed at which the students gain understanding, but the program has been tested with full classes working in sub-groups under the overall guidance of one staff member.

Reading and writing performance have been closely linked to the phonemic knowledge of the student. The use of phonemic recording is critical because it acts as a self-teaching mechanism. It enables the learner to independently identify new words and thereby acquire the orthographic representations necessary for rapid autonomous visual word recognition. Simple exposure to the alphabetic orthography is not sufficient for a child to induce alphabetic principles spontaneously.

There are basically three types of readers. There are those who read phonetically, those who read whole words, and those who use a combination of the two methods. A combination of phonics and "whole word" reading is what a good reader uses.

Poor readers may try to read phonetically but do not have the knowledge of sound–symbol correspondence to allow them to be successful. Sound-symbol correspondence must be learned before any progress will be made.

"Whole word" readers do not recognize the individual letters or groups of letters that make up a word. They look at the outside shape of the word and match this from the shapes of whole words in their memory. Their competence with reading and spelling may then be dependent on the capacity of their memory. They may know some phonics but never use them to help with reading. "Whole word" readers are thought to make up 60% of all poor readers. To improve their reading and spelling they must learn sound–symbol correspondence. Using known words and getting them to identify sounds within the words is the way to start.

The *Building Basic Literacy Skills* program can be used with all types of readers. It teaches the reading, spelling, and contextual use of single- and multi-syllable words through a systematic progression of skills. Each unit focuses on a distinct group of skills: phonic, "whole word," or syllable division methods. Teaching strategies are common throughout the program.

Building Basic Literacy Skills is a structured and sequential program that begins with the identification of vowel and consonant letters of the alphabet and quickly extends to include strategies for attempting to read and spell unknown words. It is cumulative, as each new unit draws on skills and abilities already developed and so allows for new knowledge to be incorporated into the old.

Building Basic Literacy Skills was originally written to teach strategies for reading and spelling to underachieving students of middle-school age. It is, however, suitable for all ages from nine to ninety.

Using the *Building Basic Literacy Skills* Series

These general notes should be read before following the "Procedures for Working" on page 8.

✣ Level of Knowledge Assumed

To use the *Building Basic Literacy Skills*, students need to know and be able to recite the letters of the alphabet. They need to know the basic sounds of each consonant as it occurs at the beginning of a word. They need to know the "short" sounds of each vowel. (It is helpful but not necessary for them to know the terms "vowel" and "consonant.")

✣ Organizing and Working the Program

The program is designed so that it may be delivered with a complete class of lower-ability students. More often it has been used with groups of students who have been withdrawn from mainstream classrooms. It could also, of course, be used in a one-to-one or small group tutorial situation.

While it is perfectly possible that the later reinforcement and practice exercises in each unit may be completed as homework, it is important that a tutor be on hand to provide immediate support and feedback as students work.

Many tutors have also found it beneficial for students to work with a partner, who may be at the same stage or, in some cases, in advance of their partner on the program. Discussion with other students about the tasks in question and about progress is particularly important.

The program should be overseen by certified classroom teachers, but day-to-day operation could be monitored by a support assistant. This person is referred to throughout as "the tutor."

✣ Teaching the Program

Each unit begins with guided tutor-led material. The tutor leads the discussion, always beginning from a known point and linking this with the students' previous experience and knowledge. The starting point may be reviewing the work from the previous lesson.

The tutor models any new procedure on the board, talking through the examples shown. He or she then works through the procedure together with the students. Worksheets can be photocopied onto acetate and used on an overhead projector directed onto a whiteboard. Students can then be asked to complete the worksheets on the board first before they are given independent practice. Students may work in small groups for this phase. Working with others reduces anxiety suffered by individuals as the group solves problems. The combined knowledge of the group will increase the range of expertise available to an individual student.

Once tutors are sure that the children can read and understand the instructions and tasks that follow, the students may proceed at their own pace.

The last ten minutes of each lesson are given to review and for class discussion of the work completed.

Using the *Building Basic Literacy Skills* Series *(cont.)*

✛ Reading Instructions

- Instructions boxed and marked with an "**i**" are intended, in the initial stages of the program, to be read by the tutor. They will often require demonstration to ensure that the students understand the new information. As the students progress through the program—and begin to work at their own pace—it is important that they fully understand these boxed instructions, since they introduce each new step. It is important that a tutor be on hand to check understanding and provide guidance.

- Where an "**r**" icon is included, the material in the box needs to be learned and retained by the students. The tutor might want to instruct that the students copy it into a "Spelling Rules" notebook.

- All other instructions are intended to be read, aloud if necessary, by the students themselves. Through the initial units of the program it may be helpful if the tutor checks that the students can read, understand, and follow the instructions carefully. There may also be occasions when the tutor will wish to read out the examples before the children complete the tasks. Later, students should work together, where possible, to read instructions and check understanding of sample sentences.

- Since the program is cumulative, practice in reading these instructions for themselves will help students to build up a vocabulary of basic sight words, including many of those necessary to follow instructions in other subjects. Reading these instructions for themselves also helps the students build confidence and independence and highlights the overall importance of reading and following instructions in their work.

- Single letters, vowels, or consonant blends surrounded by brackets indicate that they say their phonetic sound.

✛ Answer Key

The program is largely self-checking and typical answers for each unit are to be found on the answer pages located at the back of each book.

Since the students are actively encouraged to take control of their own learning, it may be sensible for the tutor to allow them to mark and grade their own work. This may be done by encouraging students to exchange papers to mark a partner's work. This will again involve reading and following instructions, and in itself may encourage the students to think more carefully about the patterns of letters within words.

Icon Review

| **i** | This icon indicates **instructions** to be read by the tutor. |

| **r** | This icon indicates materials that need to be learned and **retained** by the students. |

Using the *Building Basic Literacy Skills* Series *(cont.)*

Procedures for Working

Each unit should be worked through in sequential order to ensure all reading and spelling strategies are taught. The working procedures for all units are very similar and follow this progression:

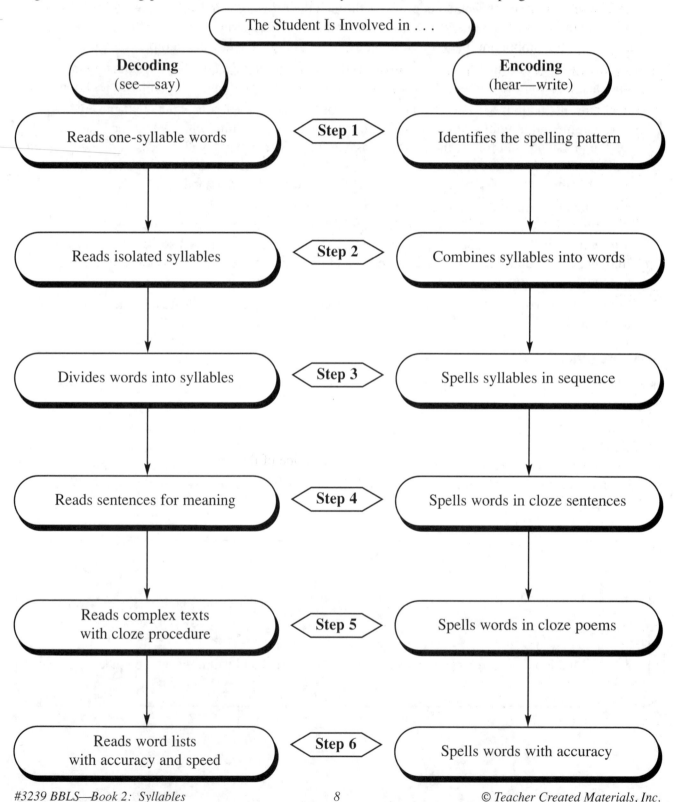

The Student Is Involved in . . .

Decoding (see—say)

Encoding (hear—write)

Decoding		Encoding
Reads one-syllable words	Step 1	Identifies the spelling pattern
Reads isolated syllables	Step 2	Combines syllables into words
Divides words into syllables	Step 3	Spells syllables in sequence
Reads sentences for meaning	Step 4	Spells words in cloze sentences
Reads complex texts with cloze procedure	Step 5	Spells words in cloze poems
Reads word lists with accuracy and speed	Step 6	Spells words with accuracy

Using the *Building Basic Literacy Skills* Series *(cont.)*

⁜ Word Lists

For reading, the goal is to teach word-attack skills so students can use them when decoding unfamiliar words. New, unfamiliar words are then included that will challenge their understanding of the strategies taught. The vocabulary is not limited. Each unit ends with Word Lists that follow the pattern of that unit. These words can be made into word cards to use for playing word games in school or at home.

The student is asked to read the Word List daily along with, or to, a peer, parent/guardian or helper. The number of words read within one minute should be plotted on a graph for that unit (provided in Appendix 1 on page 50). The graph gives a very clear indicator to the student and tutor of the improvement in the automaticity of visual word recognition.

Spelling is a more complex skill and difficult to master. The number of spellings given to learn from the word list will depend on the literacy level of the student. The words chosen should be those the students most commonly use.

Students should be questioned intermittently to check that they understand the vocabulary used in the program. The students maintain a record of their work by keeping a checklist on the Student Target Sheet. Each unit can be supplemented by using selected words from the word lists to write sentences, find their meanings in a dictionary, and find rhyming words.

⁜ Poems

The poems included towards the end of each unit have been deliberately printed in complex type. (Some non-dyslexic adults may find this makes it more difficult for them to read!) This graphic structure prevents "whole word" reading of the words and therefore activates the perceptual (right) side of the brain. Each letter has to be identified visually and so phonics comes into play.

The poems also utilize the **cloze** procedure. *Cloze*—which is sometimes called the sentence completion technique—works by deleting a word from a line of poetry and asking the students to supply the missing part. The purpose of the cloze procedure is to ensure that the student uses semantic and syntactic cues by choosing the correct word to "fit" each line of the poem. This process involves the linguistic (left) side of the brain. Pupils have to make sense of what they have read to be able to complete the poems successfully.

If pupils find reading the poems very difficult, they are asked to read the single words only. The tutor or a partner may read the poem and ask the student to "fit" the correct word into each line. The poems at the end of each unit of work can be completed as a class activity, providing opportunities for discussion.

Children and adults who read and spell with confidence have the ability to "play" with language. They can understand and take pleasure from a pun, spoonerism, or other play on words. *Building Basic Literacy Skills* endeavors to encourage this ability by including sentences and poems that are deliberately off-beat. Since many of the students will have failed already in "traditional" phonic-based approaches and may see these earlier programs as infantile, these jokes with language should be encouraged and shared. It is quite possible that in order to gain respect for the English language we also need to learn how to be a little disrespectful of it!

Using the *Building Basic Literacy Skills* Series *(cont.)*

⊹ Timed Tasks

These tasks are marked with .

The final task in each unit is intended as an assessment of what has been learned. If possible, the students should complete these tasks under pressure of time. Their aim should be to better their previous time rather than compete with other students' times. Tutors may prefer to give less able students a longer or unlimited time to complete the tasks.

⊹ Student Target Sheets

It is important that the students complete the Student Target Sheet in cooperation with the tutor as they complete each unit.

There are four different areas to be assessed:

- completion of each worksheet

- answering of questions about the topics covered

- reading speed

- spelling.

The students can color in the units completed and the rules they have remembered correctly. The results of their reading and spelling checks are recorded in the right-hand columns.

The Student Target Sheet covers the five units of the program included in the book. A certificate can be given on its successful completion.

For students of very low ability it may be sensible to mask parts of the Student Target Sheet so that they complete one unit at a time. This should keep a small number of targets within their potential grasp.

⊹ Appendices

Each book in the program contains appendices of informal assessment material to keep track of children's progress over the whole program. Appendices 1–6 may be used at any time to check a student's ability to progress through the units. Appendix 7 contains material related to each of the units.

General Guidelines for Good Practice

⇒ Familiarize yourself with the format of the program by working through the worksheets.

⇒ Take the literacy level of the students into account. Always ensure students are successful, either by limiting the amount of work to be completed, or by working through the units together.

⇒ Encourage the students to scan the whole page quickly before beginning each worksheet.

⇒ Make sure that students work in a logical manner, left to right, across the page.

⇒ Ensure that students read and follow the instructions properly.

⇒ Always encourage cursive script.

⇒ When choosing words from a list to complete a cloze passage, insist the students mark off the words as they use them.

⇒ Always encourage the re-reading of work to make sure the sentences and passages make sense.

⇒ Ensure consolidation of the phonemic pattern of letters or letter strings previously taught by frequently asking "what sound" the letters make.

⇒ The vocabulary in this program is not limited and will therefore contain some words not generally used by the students. Encourage the students to use a dictionary or spellchecker or ask for an explanation. You can use this opportunity to discuss these words with the group. (Be aware that using a dictionary may be very stressful for students with specific literacy or learning difficulties.)

⇒ Some students will always have difficulty voicing consonant blends. Do not let this hold up their progress, but place emphasis on the visual recognition of onsets.

Combining Syllables

1. Read each syllable then combine them to make words.

		Copy the word.	**Look/say/listen/cover/write/check.**
com	plete	_____	_____
col	lide	_____	_____
in	clude	_____	_____
des	cribe	_____	_____

2. Match the syllables to make a real word.

			Write the word.	**Look/say/listen/cover/write/check.**
a.	es	flate	_____	_____
	mis	treme	_____	_____
	in	cape	_____	_____
	ex	take	_____	_____

b.	com	lete	_____	_____
	ath	plete	_____	_____
	in	tume	_____	_____
	cos	vite	_____	_____

c.	ex	close	_____	_____
	en	cribe	_____	_____
	con	pose	_____	_____
	des	crete	_____	_____

3. Make sure you know what all these words mean. Use a dictionary, if needed.

Dividing Syllables

1. Divide these words into syllables (beats). (Remember: find the vowels first, mark the consonants between the vowels, then split the word into two beats.)

vc/cv	1st Beat	2nd Beat	Write the Whole Word
mistake	_____	_____	_____
describe	_____	_____	_____
explode	_____	_____	_____
combine	_____	_____	_____
excuse	_____	_____	_____
suppose	_____	_____	_____
inflate	_____	_____	_____
enclose	_____	_____	_____
include	_____	_____	_____

2. Use the words above to complete these sentences.

   a. I _____ it's my turn to make tea again.

   b. The red balloon was about to _____ with the hot air.

   c. _____ me, I was here before you!

   d. If you _____ peanut butter and chocolate, it tastes good.

   e. The bomb was about to _____.

   f. Please _____ a stamped, addressed envelope.

   g. The man had to _____ his stolen car to the policeman.

   h. I would like you to _____ me in your plans to go out.

   i. Why do I always make a _____ with my spelling?

Endings that Begin with a Vowel

1. Add *ed* or *ing* to the silent *e* words. (Remember to take off the silent *e* first, if necessary.) Then complete the sentences so they make sense.

   a. I was being chase _____ by _____ so I
      _____.

   b. The bus will be arrive _____ at _____ if I do not
      _____ I shall miss it.

   c. My red dress fade _____. Now my socks are _____.

   d. She blame _____ me for _____ when I
      _____.

   e. She was refuse _____ to _____ so I
      _____.

2. Underline, then correct, the two spelling mistakes in each sentence. Then add two sentences to finish the story.

   I am saveing up to buy some skats. I am hopping one day to be a

   skateing star. I would be licked by all my fanns. They would yell for me

   when iam ussing my skates. I cannot wait to be speedeing around the ice

   like an athleete. I will get the bigest priz on earth! My mom hops I will

   get married and have children but I _____

   _____

   _____

   _____

   _____

　　　　14

Endings that Begin with a Consonant

> **i** Do not take off the silent *e* if the suffix (ending) begins with a consonant.

1. The blends *ment*, *ful*, and *less* are suffixes. Choose one of these endings to add to each base word so it makes sense.

   use _____   base_____   state_____

   grate _____   hope _____   life_____

   pave _____   waste _____   home_____

   use _____   blame _____   hope_____

2. Delete the words not needed in the following sentences.

   a. The gravy was **taste tasting tasteless**.

   b. The man was **hoped hopeful hopeless** he would win the race.

   c. I am **blame blameless blamed**. It was Tim who broke the jug.

   d. That was a silly **state statement stating** you have just made!

3. Choose two of these suffixes—*er*, *less*, *ing*, and *est*—to add to each base word so it makes sense. Write the two new words.

   safe   _____   _____

   smoke   _____   _____

   take   _____   _____

   ripe   _____   _____

   late   _____   _____

   explore   _____   _____

   intrude   _____   _____

Silent "e" Poetry

Read the words in the box. Then use them to complete each line of the poems.

1.
| tasteful — plateful — ungrateful — wasteful |

I think you're so _____

Not to eat this tasty_____.

It is just so _____

When this dinner is so_____.

2.
| impede — inflate — stampede — state |

Everyone was in a _____

The balloon was about to over-_____.

The balloon grew so big it did _____

On the people—so they started a _____.

3.
| intrude — dictate — crude — escape |

Teachers confuse me, so I try to _____

When they find me, they make me _____.

I try to ignore them but they always _____

"You write this down and stop being _____."

Unit 1 Word List

 Say the sound of the underlined letters, then read the words. Read across the page from left to right. How many words can you read in one minute?

concrete	invite	suppose	include
confuse	impede	compose	trombone
capsule	excuse	implore	supreme
cascade	translate	empire	escape
incline	oppose	intrude	stampede
concave	obtuse	compose	pollute
explore	costume	inflate	extreme
collide	ignore	immune	inhale
inquire	explode	enclose	describe
dictate	postpone	enzyme	capsule
upgrade	nickname	update	advise
despite	incline	subside	subscribe
compute	exclude	consume	mundane
described	safest	chased	ignored
refused	arrived	latest	inhaler

Which word from the list above means "to ask"? _____

Two Vowels in One Syllable.

> **i** Reminder: When two vowels go out walking in one syllable, the first one does the talking and says its name. The second vowel says nothing.

1. Say the sound of the underlined vowels then read the word.

s<u>ee</u>	t<u>oe</u>	s<u>oa</u>p	d<u>ay</u>	s<u>ai</u>l
t<u>ie</u>	bl<u>ue</u>	k<u>ee</u>p	l<u>oa</u>d	cr<u>ea</u>m
m<u>ai</u>l	<u>ea</u>st	st<u>ay</u>	gl<u>ue</u>	b<u>oa</u>t
b<u>ea</u>k	g<u>ee</u>se	cl<u>ay</u>	dr<u>ai</u>n	c<u>ue</u>
fl<u>oa</u>t	ch<u>ai</u>n	scr<u>ee</u>n	sw<u>ay</u>	<u>oa</u>th
d<u>ie</u>	scr<u>ea</u>m	ch<u>ee</u>r	r<u>ea</u>ch	thr<u>oa</u>t

2. Use the words above to complete the sentences.

a. I nearly choked when the toast stuck in my _____.

b. The _____ on the boat was flapping in the wind.

c. Dad put sugar and _____ in his coffee.

d. The postman collects the _____ every day but Sunday.

e. I put the spider on her hair and waited for the _____.

f. I stubbed my _____ on the brick near the gate.

g. The gum stuck like _____ on my dress.

h. She washed her hands with _____ and water.

i. The sun rises in the _____ .

j. The _____ on my bike had jammed.

18

Adding Endings

1. Study the words below then fill in the blanks with the correct word.

bead	beads		beading
stain		stained	
	greets		greeting
			cheering
load		loaded	loading
	floats	floated	
		stayed	staying
cheat	cheats		cheating
	heats	heated	

2. Add *s*, *ing*, or *ed* to one word so each sentence makes sense. Write the new sentence on the line provided.

a. The cat was creep along the wall.

_____

b. Tom need to mend his bike.

_____

c. My mom always greet me with a kiss. Ugh!

_____

d. My dad was speed in his car.

_____

e. The two sleeve were rolled up on his shirt.

_____

f. The song finished and everyone cheer.

_____

g. I think you cheat on your exam.

_____

h. The boat were lined up in the dock.

_____

Two-Vowel Words

1. Write four words that rhyme with the following words.

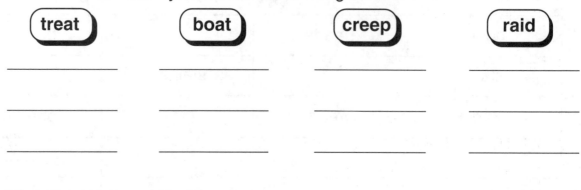

treat	boat	creep	raid

_____   _____   _____   _____

_____   _____   _____   _____

_____   _____   _____   _____

_____   _____   _____   _____

2. Fill in the missing vowels to complete the following words. Use *ee*, *oa*, and *ai*. Make sure that no two words are the same.

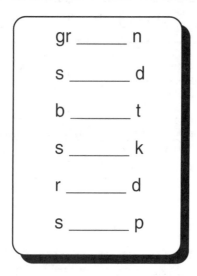

gr _____ n
s _____ d
b _____ t
s _____ k
r _____ d
s _____ p

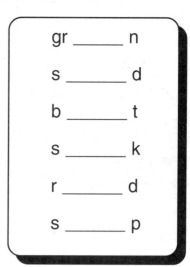

gr _____ n
s _____ d
b _____ t
s _____ k
r _____ d
s _____ p

3. Cross out the word or words that are not needed in each of the following sentences.

a. The toad began to **creak croak** as he jumped into the moat.

b. It was a **trait treat** to shop on Fleet Street.

c. The bandit went to **raid read** the comic book store.

d. Do not **mean moan** about your homework.

e. The **breed braid** in her hair is **grain green**.

f. The cake had grated orange **pail peel** in it, and it got stuck in my teeth.

Edit and Revise

1. Add *ing* or *ed* to words in each sentence of the story so it makes sense. Complete the story in your own words.

Her finger was bleed so I put a bandage on it. She was scream so much she said she felt like faint. As she spoke she keel over and landed in an open drain at the side of the path. She was now soak wet and she smell horribly. She began screech. I thought she had been maim for life but she had only _____

_____

_____.

2. Match the words in present tense to those in past tense. Then use each word to complete the sentences below.

Present tense	Past tense
lay	laid
say	said
pay	paid

a. I _____ my keys on the table when I get home from school.

b. Yesterday, I _____ two quarters on my desk. Now I can't find them!

c. I _____ 70 cents to buy two candy bars at school the other day.

d. Tomorrow, I will _____ 75 cents to ride the bus.

e. If they ask me to go, I will _____, "No, thank you!"

f. He _____ I had to give him his book back.

Two-Vowel Poetry

Read the words then use them to complete each line of the poems.

1.
float — moat — boat — throat

Did **you** know th**at I** can _____?

So **I** don't n**ee**d to buy **a**_____.

I'll j**ump** str**aight** in and sw**i**m **the** _____.

I h**o**pe **I** d**o**n't get **a fro**g stuck in my_____.

2.
train — chain — drain — rain

I wa**s** standing in th**e** _____

Jus**t** waiti**n**g f**or the** 11:00_____

Whe**n I** lo**st my** silv**er** _____.

It just went d**o**wn th**e** _____!

3.
scream — cream — weasels — measels

Di**d** y**o**u k**n**ow that t**h**e _____

Is a **d**isease that atta**c**ks _____?

If y**o**u're squeamish, **p**le**a**se **do**n't _____

Bu**t they** eat de**a**d frogs **c**overed in _____.

Unit 2 Word List

 Say the underlined vowel sounds then read the words. Read across the page from left to right. How many words can you read in one minute?

s<u>ee</u>	<u>ai</u>d	t<u>ea</u>	d<u>ay</u>
<u>oa</u>t	f<u>ee</u>	f<u>ai</u>l	b<u>ea</u>k
pl<u>ay</u>	g<u>oa</u>t	ch<u>ea</u>p	h<u>ai</u>l
fr<u>ea</u>k	tr<u>ay</u>	cl<u>oa</u>k	bl<u>ee</u>d
f<u>ai</u>nt	bl<u>ea</u>ch	sw<u>ay</u>	thr<u>oa</u>t
wh<u>ee</u>ze	r<u>ai</u>se	pl<u>ea</u>d	sl<u>ay</u>
sh<u>ee</u>t	br<u>ai</u>n	dr<u>ea</u>m	pr<u>ay</u>
t<u>oa</u>st	bl<u>ee</u>d	pr<u>ai</u>se	pl<u>ea</u>t
cl<u>ay</u>	b<u>oa</u>st	sw<u>ee</u>t	gl<u>ea</u>m
p<u>ay</u>	s<u>oa</u>k	b<u>ee</u>ch	b<u>ea</u>ch
bl<u>ea</u>ch	l<u>oa</u>f	l<u>ea</u>f	cr<u>oa</u>k
b<u>oa</u>t	k<u>ee</u>n	g<u>ee</u>se	t<u>ea</u>m
s<u>ee</u>m	s<u>ea</u>m	tw<u>ee</u>d	scr<u>ee</u>n
fr<u>ee</u>ze	spr<u>ai</u>n	f<u>ai</u>th	p<u>ai</u>nt
h<u>ea</u>ve	<u>oa</u>k	sn<u>ai</u>l	tr<u>ai</u>l

There are five different vowel patterns in the list above. Name them.

_____ _____ _____ _____ _____

The V/CV Pattern

> **i** Some two-syllable words only have one consonant between the vowels so the word is split before the consonant:
>
> music — mu / sic
>
> The vowel of the first syllable is open, so it says its name.

1. These words have been split for you. Read each syllable and listen for the word. Then look, say, listen, cover, write, and check!

be	gin	_____		bo	nus	_____
mu	sic	_____		hu	man	_____
la	dy	_____		fi	nal	_____
o	ver	_____		ze	ro	_____

2. Now find the syllables of the following words. Mark the vowels, and then divide the words into syllables using the v/cv pattern.

vc/cv	1st Syllable	2nd Syllable	Write the Whole Word
moment	_____	_____	_____
chosen	_____	_____	_____
minus	_____	_____	_____
taken	_____	_____	_____
remote	_____	_____	_____
gravy	_____	_____	_____
item	_____	_____	_____
Friday	_____	_____	_____

3. Read the words again.

24

Matching Syllables

1. Read the syllables and match them up to make a word. Then look, say, listen, cover, write, and check!

a.

o	sic	_____
di	ly	_____
mu	man	_____
Ju	ver	_____
hu	rect	_____

b.

gra	vil	_____
e	nal	_____
fi	vy	_____
va	ber	_____
so	cant	_____

c.

bru	val	_____
le	tal	_____
ba	gal	_____
ro	con	_____
o	bot	_____

d.

se	pid	_____
stu	bic	_____
slo	cret	_____
fe	gan	_____
cu	ver	_____

2. Choose from the words above to complete each sentence.

a. I ate _____ and eggs for breakfast.

b. I like _____ on my mashed potatoes.

c. A robot is not a _____ being.

d. You must always keep a _____.

e. I will _____ you onto the right path.

f. If you feel hot and ill, you may have a _____.

g. The U.S. president's office has an _____ shape.

h. I like pop _____ better than rap.

Words Ending in "al"

1. Add the letters *al* to complete the second syllable. Combine the syllables to find the word. Then look, say, listen, cover, write, and check!

   fin _____   _____   loc_____   _____

   equ _____   _____   brut _____   _____

   leg _____   _____   riv _____   _____

   tot _____   _____   spin _____   _____

2. Complete the sentences using the words above.

   a. The _____ news and weather forecast can be found on TV.

   b. The shopping bill came to a _____ of $88.76.

   c. To make a cake, you need _____ amounts of sugar and flour.

   d. Carl has a _____ who is interested in his girlfriend.

   e. The _____ man kicked the dog out of his way.

   f. Fortunately, he didn't damage his _____ cord in the accident.

   g. The _____ lap of the race will be worth watching.

3. Look at the words below. Then complete the blanks by following the pattern.

final		finally
		equally
local		
	totals	

4. Now read the words.

26   © *Teacher Created Materials, Inc.*

Types of Syllables

> **i** **Open syllables** end in one vowel. The vowel says its name.
> **Closed-in syllables** have one vowel and end in a consonant. The vowel says its short sound.
> **r** **Silent *e* syllables** have one vowel followed by one consonant, followed by *e*. The vowel says its name.

1. Underline the vowels in the following words. Look at the syllables. Decide which sort of syllable they are, and then write each syllable under the correct heading below. The first syllables have been placed for you.

   fa – tal   re – tire   ar – rive   re – late   in – trude

   pri – vate   si – lent   e – ven   stu – pid   com – plete

Ends with a Vowel: Open Syllable	Vowel Closed In by a Consonant: Closed-in Syllable	Last Syllable of the Word, Ends in *e*: Silent *e* Syllable
fa	tal	

2. Use a word from above to complete each sentence.

   a. The child did not say anything. He was _____.

   b. Two is an _____ number.

   c. I wish to _____ from work at sixty years of age.

   d. Do not _____ late for the funeral service.

   e. Please _____ your work and then hand it in to me.

Syllables Ending with a Vowel Poetry

Read the words then use them to complete each line of the poems.

1. | insect — object — protect — dissect |

In science class, we **had to** _____

A **little tiny** blue and black _____.

I **felt** so **bad; I wanted** to _____

That poor **little** thing. I had to _____.

2. | decline — cosine — define — Caroline |

In Englsh class, **we** ha**d to** _____

The mathematical term _____.

Bu**t a** stubborn girl **named** _____

Shook her head and **d said, "I** _____."

3. | over — Rover — crazy — lazy |

Why are **you** so _____?

You **must** be completely _____.

Your exams will soon be _____

Then you **can** nap **with your dog,** _____.

28

Unit 3 Word List

 Read the underlined syllables then practice reading and spelling the words. (The first syllable is an open syllable and so the vowel will say its name.) How many words can you read in one minute?

begin	began	remote	refine
demon	omit	direct	cupid
stupid	music	focus	bonus
human	tulip	cubic	July
widen	oval	even	gravy
evil	Venus	vocal	rival
index	lazy	crazy	zero
taken	basic	item	able
desire	label	direct	silent
final	defy	slogan	prepare
open	pilot	solo	select
equip	equate	over	delete
severe	deplete	begun	reduce
deflate	primate	became	fatal
hotel	pupil	humid	unit

Which of the words above means "to use up or exhaust"? _____

"Robin Words"

> **i** When one consonant or consonant blend is between two vowels, try v/cv first. However, look at these words: *robin, prison, method, limit*. If we put the slash (/) after the vowel, it would make the vowel say its name! In these words, divide after the consonant vc/v. This will make the vowel say its short sound because the vowel is "closed in."
> Examples: *rob/in, pris/on, lim/it*

1. Combine the syllables to make a real word. Then look, say, listen, cover, write, and check!

   gren ade _____   sev en _____

   val id _____   sol id _____

   riv er _____   lim it _____

   men u _____   lem on _____

   pris on _____   pan ic _____

2. Choose one of the words to complete each sentence.

   a. There are _____ days in a week.

   b. The warranty was not _____ because it was out of date.

   c. When the robbers entered the bank, we all began to_____.

   d. The ducks were swimming down the _____.

   e. People who do wrong are locked up in _____.

   f. I _____ myself to three chips; otherwise I would eat them all.

   g. There are three states of matter: _____, liquid, and gas.

   h. Our school _____ includes a salad with everything.

   i. The soldier took out the hand- _____ and hurled it at the tank.

Dividing VC/V Syllables

1. Divide the following words into two syllables, using vc/v.

vc/cv	1st Syllable	2nd Syllable	Cover and Write the Word
polish	_____	_____	_____
travel	_____	_____	_____
lemon	_____	_____	_____
ever	_____	_____	_____
clever	_____	_____	_____
solid	_____	_____	_____
vanish	_____	_____	_____
never	_____	_____	_____
comic	_____	_____	_____

2. Read the following. Then match the syllables to make a real word.

a.

met	im	_____
den	en	_____
fin	al	_____
clev	ish	_____
lin	er	_____

b.

cred	apt	_____
ad	en	_____
tal	it	_____
lem	ent	_____
sev	on	_____

c.

riv	ic	_____
pan	ish	_____
mel	el	_____
rad	er	_____
grav	on	_____

d.

hab	il	_____
ev	en	_____
sliv	it	_____
men	er	_____
giv	u	_____

Verb Sense

Add *ing* and *ed* to the verb. Then use one of the words to complete each sentence. The first one has been done for you.

1. polish _____polished_____   _____polishing_____

   The man was _____polishing_____ the table top.

   The man _____polished_____ the table top.

2. finish _____   _____

   I was just _____ my dinner when there was a knock on the front door.

   I had just _____ my dinner when there was a knock on the front door.

3. adapt _____   _____

   The TV man _____ the channels to pick up satellite TV.

   The TV man was _____ the channels to pick up satellite TV.

4. promise _____   _____

   My dad _____ to buy me a bike for my birthday.

   My dad was _____ to buy me a bike for my birthday.

5. travel _____   _____

   The bus was _____ at 30 miles per hour through the shopping center.

   The bus _____ at 30 miles per hour through the shopping center.

Words Ending with "ic" and "ish"

> ℹ️ Words with more than one syllable that end with the sound /ik/ are spelled *ic*.

1. Add *ic* or *ish* to the syllables below to make a real word. Then look, say, listen, cover, write, and check!

   clin _____ _____   com_____ _____

   van _____ _____   pun _____ _____

   frol _____ _____   rad _____ _____

   stat _____ _____   mim_____ _____

   fin _____ _____   pol_____ _____

   trop_____ _____   ep _____ _____

2. Match these meanings to the words above. The first has been done for you.

   a. kids' magazine _____ comic _____

   b. red vegetable _____

   c. disappear _____

   d. not moving _____

   e. end _____

   f. copy someone's voice _____

   g. cause pain to someone _____

   h. just north or south of the equator _____

   i. have fun _____

   j. to make clean and shiny _____

   k. very long book or film _____

   l. place to get medical help _____

Using "Robin Words"

1. Choose the best word to complete the sentence. Then cross out the others. Be careful to look for the base words.

   a. The man was **polish polished polishing** the windows.

   b. Ms. Gill will **travel travels traveling** around the world next year.

   c. Jenny is **study studying** at Blackburn College this year.

   d. Odd socks seem to be **vanish vanished vanishing** after every wash.

   e. The room was **panel panels paneled** in oak. It looked very grand.

   f. I shall be **visit visited visiting** my family at Christmas.

2. Underline the "robin words" as you read the story. Complete the story using your own words.

   The tenor was singing so high that a button shot from his cravat and landed on a radish on someone's plate of salad. His face went red and shriveled. It was comical. I wasn't the only one who started laughing. I couldn't help it. The man finished his tribute to Elvis and then vanished from the stage.

   I just _____

   _____

   _____ .

3. Write the "robin words" on the lines below.

   _____   _____   _____

   _____   _____   _____

   _____   _____   _____

   _____

"Robin Words" Poetry

1. | ever — muddy — clever — study |

    I **work** har**d to be** _____.

    I read f**o**r**e**ver and _____.

    But **I** fo**u**nd t**h**at too much _____.

    Ma**kes** my p**oo**r brain _____.

2. | camel — travel — gravel— mammal |

    W**o**uld **you** li**k**e to **ride** o**n a** _____?

    Wi**th** a **h**ump, i**t**'s quite a**n** od**d** _____.

    They'll **cross** sand o**r** dirt o**r**_____.

    Someti**mes**, it's t**h**e **best** way to _____.

3. | rivet — pivot — attic — static |

    The**re was a man who went t**o **the** _____.

    He **saw a ghost; his hair** we**n**t _____.

    He ran **downstairs and** then did **a**_____.

    He **n**ailed t**h**e **door** with **a** steel _____.

Unit 4 Word List

 Read the underlined syllable then practice reading and spelling the words. (Remember to read across the page from left to right.) How many words can you read in one minute?

<u>a</u>tom	<u>co</u>met	<u>te</u>nor	<u>me</u>nu
<u>li</u>ly	<u>liv</u>id	<u>ro</u>bin	<u>mo</u>del
<u>pro</u>per	<u>top</u>ic	<u>tro</u>pic	<u>cop</u>y
<u>com</u>ic	<u>pol</u>ish	<u>bo</u>dy	<u>sol</u>id
<u>vo</u>lume	<u>proj</u>ect	<u>no</u>vel	<u>mod</u>ern
<u>pro</u>duct	<u>stu</u>dy	<u>pun</u>ish	<u>riv</u>er
<u>wi</u>dow	<u>lin</u>en	<u>mim</u>ic	<u>sliv</u>er
<u>pi</u>vot	<u>ven</u>om	<u>meth</u>od	<u>vis</u>it
<u>pri</u>son	<u>fin</u>ish	<u>trib</u>ute	<u>sev</u>en
<u>met</u>al	<u>den</u>im	<u>tep</u>id	<u>mel</u>on
<u>cred</u>it	<u>nev</u>er	<u>pre</u>sent	<u>clev</u>er
<u>lem</u>on	<u>ped</u>al	<u>lev</u>el	<u>plan</u>et
<u>rig</u>id	<u>mod</u>el	<u>gre</u>nade	<u>val</u>id
<u>tal</u>ent	<u>cam</u>el	<u>pan</u>el	<u>grav</u>el
<u>mag</u>ic	<u>rad</u>ish	<u>stat</u>ic	<u>prof</u>it

1. Circle the words that rhyme with *ever*. How many are there? _____

Charting "r" Words

> **i** When *r* follows one vowel, together they make one sound.
> - **er** ➤ *hammer* (sound: /ur/)
> - **ir** ➤ *bird:* (sound: /ur/)
> - **ur** ➤ *church:* (sound: /ur/)
> - **ar** ➤ *cart:* (sound: /ar/)
> - **or** ➤ *fork:* (sound: /or/)

Underline the vowels that have *r* after them. Then look, say, listen, cover, write, and check, putting the words into the correct list.

church	card	her	smart	bird	hurt
cork	turn	term	thorn	burn	skirt
form	bark	north	fern	born	dart
mark	herb	sharp	herd	short	birth
third	flirt	churn	perm	burst	first

er	ir	ur	or	ar

Matching "r" Syllables

1. Match the syllables to make a real word. Then look, say, listen, cover, write, and check!

a.

but	ver	_____
whis	der	_____
an	ter	_____
thun	ger	_____
sil	per	_____

b.

bet	ner	_____
tem	mer	_____
ham	per	_____
num	ter	_____
din	ber	_____

c.

par	ber	_____
art	der	_____
spi	lor	_____
gar	ist	_____
bar	den	_____

d.

ser	by	_____
per	tain	_____
cer	vant	_____
der	dict	_____
ver	son	_____

e.

thir	phan	_____
ab	ty	_____
for	ford	_____
af	est	_____
or	sorb	_____

f.

ur	mur	_____
mur	prise	_____
fur	turb	_____
sur	ban	_____
dis	nish	_____

2. Look back and check your spellings. Check to be sure that you know what each word means.

Dividing "r" Syllables

1. Keeping *ir*, *er*, *ur*, *or*, and *ar* together, divide the following words into two syllables using vc/cv or v/cv patterns.

vc/cv	1st Syllable	2nd Syllable	Write the Whole Word
dirty	_____	_____	_____
perfect	_____	_____	_____
formal	_____	_____	_____
curtsy	_____	_____	_____
darling	_____	_____	_____
thirty	_____	_____	_____
absorb	_____	_____	_____
turnip	_____	_____	_____
expert	_____	_____	_____
remark	_____	_____	_____
sober	_____	_____	_____

2. Use the words above to complete these sentences.

   a. My dad ate a carrot and a _____.

   b. My aunt turns _____ on her next birthday.

   c. Girls sometimes _____ after the final act of a show.

   d. I do not know anyone who is _____.

   e. Paper towels _____ liquid very quickly.

   f. Dress was _____ at the party, so I did not wear my jeans.

   g. I am an _____ on my computer.

Rhymes with "ore"

> **i** Words with *ore* rhyme with *sore*.

1. Write out these words with *ore* as their ending sound. Look, say, listen, cover, write, and check!

   more _____   core _____   sore _____

   snore _____   swore _____   before _____

   tore _____   score _____   implore _____

   ignore _____

2. Use the words above to complete the blanks in the story below.

   The football game was very slow. There was no _____,
   and the man next to me began to _____. He was
   asleep! I was surprised to the _____. My throat was
   _____ from shouting. When we lost the game, I
   _____ I would never go to any _____ football
   games again. I will _____ my friends who
   _____ me to support my team. I actually
   _____ up my season ticket. _____ you say
   anything, it was last year's ticket!

3. Study the words and complete the blanks to fit the pattern.

snore		snoring
	scored	
		ignoring

40

Rhymes with "are"

> **i** Words with *are* rhyme with *hair*.

1. Write out these words with *are* as their ending sound. Look, say, listen, cover, write, and check!

   bare _____   square _____   share _____

   stare _____   compare _____   beware _____

   care _____   glare _____   scare _____

   fare _____   declare _____   prepare _____

2. Use the words above to complete the blanks in the sentences below.

   a. The ghost in that movie didn't _____ me.

   b. Basic shapes include circle, _____ , and triangle.

   c. Don't _____ at the sun during an eclipse.

   d. She tried to _____ dinner before 6:00.

   e. The sign read, "_____ of the guard dog."

3. Study the words and complete the blanks to fit the pattern.

declare		declaring
	shared	
		glaring

Double "r" Words

When a word has two *r*'s together, the vowels do not join with the *r*, they say their own sound.

1. Read each syllable then combine them to make words.

		Copy the word	**Look/say/listen/cover/write/check**
car	ry	_____	_____
hur	ry	_____	_____
squir	rel	_____	_____
ber	ry	_____	_____
ar	rive	_____	_____
hor	ror	_____	_____
cher	ry	_____	_____
er	ror	_____	_____

2. Match the syllables to make a real word.

a.

hor	rant	_____
mir	rot	_____
cur	rid	_____
car	ror	_____

b.

ter	rot	_____
quar	rect	_____
par	ror	_____
cor	rel	_____

The Letter "r" Poetry

Read the words then use them to complete each line of the poems.

1. | term — letter — better — germ |

I caught this awful _____

During the last school _____.

My mother wrote the school a_____

Saying I'd return when I felt _____.

2. | fur — spider — error — terror |

The old lady was filled with _____

When she realized her _____.

It was not a stain on her coat of _____

But a big fat hairy _____.

3. | cherry — garden — pardon — carry |

I said to the farmer, "I beg your _____,

But where is the vegetable _____?

"Look for the sign with a big red _____.

You'll find produce—all you can _____."

Unit 5 Word List

 Say the sound of the underlined letters then practice reading and spelling the words. (Remember to read across the page from left to right.) How many words can you read in one minute?

h<u>er</u>	f<u>or</u>m	m<u>ar</u>k	op<u>er</u>a
sm<u>ar</u>t	nect<u>ar</u>	b<u>or</u>n	fl<u>ir</u>t
mod<u>er</u>n	<u>or</u>gan	f<u>ir</u>st	ang<u>er</u>
must<u>ar</u>d	hung<u>er</u>	sk<u>ir</u>t	rep<u>or</u>t
min<u>or</u>	thund<u>er</u>	b<u>ur</u>st	buzz<u>er</u>
sob<u>er</u>	pref<u>er</u>	M<u>ar</u>ch	p<u>er</u>son
suff<u>er</u>	abs<u>or</u>b	mot<u>or</u>	bak<u>er</u>
numb<u>er</u>	lett<u>er</u>	rep<u>or</u>t	f<u>or</u>mal
rid<u>er</u>	rubb<u>er</u>	f<u>or</u>ty	gl<u>are</u>
wint<u>er</u>	sist<u>er</u>	m<u>or</u>ning	decl<u>are</u>
p<u>er</u>fect	aff<u>or</u>d	m<u>ir</u>r<u>or</u>	dinn<u>er</u>
inf<u>or</u>m	comp<u>are</u>	t<u>err</u>or	c<u>are</u>
ch<u>err</u>y	squ<u>are</u>	<u>err</u>or	sh<u>are</u>
b<u>are</u>	b<u>err</u>y	h<u>or</u>rid	bew<u>are</u>
st<u>are</u>	<u>ar</u>rive	c<u>or</u>k	c<u>ar</u>rot

Using Student Target Sheets

❖ Completed Worksheets

After receiving marked worksheets, students can color in the appropriate square or squares on their sheet under "Completed Work." For example, if pages 12 and 18 have been completed, then the boxes relating to pages 12 and 18 are colored in. Marking should be strict. Students handing in incomplete pages should not be allowed to color in the target. This will encourage students to ask for help if they are having difficulties and will discourage sloppy work.

❖ Oral Assessment

While students are completing a task they can be checked for their understanding of the work that has been covered. The questions to be asked for each target follow these instructions. For any correct answer the appropriate rectangle should be colored in immediately on their Target Sheet.

Tutors can use their discretion as to how much help they give to students to enable them to complete a target. Help should be given in the form of modeling. The tutor completes an activity relating to the target question, then asks the student that same question. If the student is successful then he or she has completed that target and it may be colored in.

The tutor can use the information gained from the students' answers to find which areas need more attention and explanation. These may be addressed as a whole-class activity or with individual students.

❖ Reading Targets

The targets set for reading are based on speed and should be set according to the literacy level of the group or individual; and they must be attainable. It may be more appropriate just to record the number of words read in a certain time (e.g., 60 seconds) rather than give a definite speed for reading.

Pupils reading the word lists at home can keep an accurate record of their reading by filling in a graph (see Appendix 1 on pages 49 and 50). This will show a clear record of the increase in their speed of reading.

❖ Spelling Targets

The target words set for spelling should, if possible, be words the students will tend to use. The number of words given is at the discretion of the tutor.

❖ Appropriateness

The Student Target Sheets may not be suitable for those with very low literacy skills. It is left to the discretion of the tutor whether to use them or not.

Tutor's Instructions for Student Target Sheet

page 12	Where would you look to find out the meaning of a word? (*in a dictionary*)
page 15	What do you have to remember when you add suffixes "less," "ful," or "ment" to a silent *e* word? (*do not take off the "e" if the suffix begins witih a consonant*)
page 18	When two vowels are next to each other in a syllable, what does the first vowel usually say? (*its name*)
page 18	When two vowels are next to each other in a word, what does the second vowel usually say? (*nothing*)
page 24	Where would you break up the word "human" into two syllables? (*in front of the "m" : "hu/man"*)
page 27	A syllable that ends with a vowel is called an "open" syllable. What does the vowel sound like in an "open" syllable? (*The vowel says its name.*)
page 30	If you have only one consonant between two vowels—for example in the word "robin"—and you use the v/cv rule and it does not give you a word, what do you do? (*split the word up after the consonant: "rob/in"*)
page 33	The /ik/ sound in the word "pick" is spelled "ick." How do you spell the /ik/ sound in "picnic" and other words that have more than one syllable and end in the sound /ik/? (*ic*)
page 37	If the letter "r" follows a vowel, what do you have to remember? (*The "r" sticks to the vowel and together they give one sound.*)
page 37	Three vowels, when placed before the letter "r" say the same sound: /ur/. Which three vowels are they? (*"e," "i," and "u"*)
page 41	What sound do the letters "are" give in a word? Think of the words "care" and "fare." (*In words, "are" sounds like "air."*)

46

Student Target Sheet

Name: _____   Date started: _____

Completed work	I know . . .	Reading	Spelling
Unit 1	**Two-Syllable Words**	I can read _____ words in _____ seconds.	I can spell _____ out of _____.
page 12	to use a dictionary to find words I do not know the meaning of.		
page 15	not to take off the "e" when adding a suffix that begins with a consonant.		
Unit 2	**Two Vowels Together**	I can read _____ words in _____ seconds.	I can spell _____ out of _____.
page 18	when two vowels are together in one syllable the first vowel says its name.		
page 18	when two vowels are together in one syllable the second vowel says nothing.		
Unit 3	**Syllables Ending with a Vowel**	I can read _____ words in _____ seconds.	I can spell _____ out of _____.
page 24	if a word has one consonant between two vowels then you break it after the first vowel.		
page 27	that open syllables end in a vowel that says its name.		
Unit 4	**VC/V Words**	I can read _____ words in _____ seconds.	I can spell _____ out of _____.
page 30	that if you have split up a word v/cv and this does not give you a word, then divide the word after the consonant.		
page 33	that words that have more than one syllable and end with the sound (ik) are spelled "ic."		
Unit 5	**Vowels Followed by "r"**	I can read _____ words in _____ seconds.	I can spell _____ out of _____.
page 37	when one "r" follows a vowel they join together to give one sound.		
page 37	"er," "ur," and "ir" all say the same sound: /ur/.		
page 41	when "e" follows "ar," it says /air/.		

CERTIFICATE OF ACHIEVEMENT

Awarded to

For successfully completing Units 1–5 of the Building Basic Literacy Skills program

_____
Signature

_____
Date

48

Graph of Reading Speed

Ask the students to read the Word List on the last page of the unit being worked on every day. They should count the number of words read in one minute and put a mark on the graph for that unit to indicate this number. You may need to provide the student with several copies of the graph for each unit, depending on the number of sessions taken to complete it.

The completed graphs will give a clear indication of progress and will motivate the student. It is important to encourage the students to become familiar with reading accurately under pressure as this is what is expected of them during their internal and external exams.

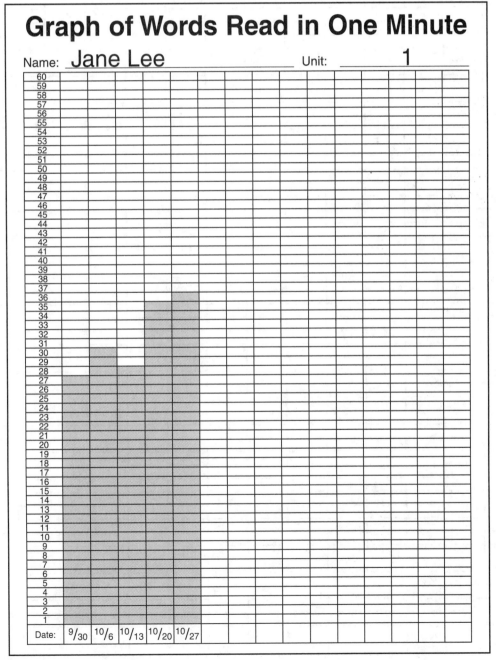

Graph of Words Read in One Minute

Name: _____ Unit: _____

60													
59													
58													
57													
56													
55													
54													
53													
52													
51													
50													
49													
48													
47													
46													
45													
44													
43													
42													
41													
40													
39													
38													
37													
36													
35													
34													
33													
32													
31													
30													
29													
28													
27													
26													
25													
24													
23													
22													
21													
20													
19													
18													
17													
16													
15													
14													
13													
12													
11													
10													
9													
8													
7													
6													
5													
4													
3													
2													
1													
Date:													

The "Self Voice" Method

The "self voice" is likened to the voice we hear inside our heads when we are concentrating intently on information given verbally: We sub-vocalize what we hear. We can try to recreate this "concentration" with the students by using a tape recorder to record themselves reading and then listening to the tape.

Any spelling that is causing a problem can be recorded onto a tape and then listened to. The procedure for this is as follows:

1. The words to learn are identified from the word lists and errors found in class work. (The number of words given will depend on the literacy level of each student.)

2. The student reads the word to the tutor. The tutor ensures that the pronunciation of the word is correct.

3. The student reads the whole word onto tape, then reads the name of each letter that makes up the word while tracing over the word with a pen. (Count to three silently while the tape is on record between each word to ensure that the student can easily recognize the end of each word.)

4. The tape is rewound.

5. The student listens to a word and the letter names; he or she then pauses the tape and writes down the spelling of the word. All the words are listened to and written down in this way.

It is important to encourage the student to wait until the end of the naming of the letters of a word before he or she writes down the letters. This brings in a memory element to the procedure.

Students can listen to the tape as many times as they wish. They may also record just the whole word on the reverse side of the tape and then check their own spelling knowledge if they wish to.

Be aware that a student may mix up the letter names with the incorrect shapes. To check his, ask the student to write down the shapes of the letters as you recite the letter names from A to Z.

Phonic Spell Checks

A check of non-real words can be made on the phonic knowledge of students by giving them spell checks. The words are non-real so the students will have to use their knowledge of phonics to attempt to spell the words (auditory to orthographic).

The students can also be asked to read the words to check their visual phonetic knowledge.

✢ Phonic Spell Check for Short Vowels and Single Consonants

The words below and on page 53 can be photocopied onto cardstock to make word cards. After working through Unit 1, ask each student to read these **cvc** words. Use the "Phonic Checklist" (Appendix 4, page 55) to keep a record of sounds known.

tud	fug
yem	quot
hul	bup

Phonic Spell Checks *(cont.)*

nal	cas
gox	sut
wat	kef
noz	wiv
mib	maz
ris	vek

Phonic Checklist

After giving the non-real word spell check, mark on the checklist all of the single consonants and vowels the student has successfully identified. Sound cards should be made of any letters not known by the student. (See Appendix 6 on page 59.)

Phonic Checklist *(cont.)*

Name:_____

	Spelled	Read		Spelled	Read		Spelled	Read
a			x			ch		
b			y			sh		
c			z			th		
d			bl			nh		
e			cl			ct		
f			fl			nt		
g			gl			lf		
h			pl			ck		
i			sl			ss		
j			br			ft		
k			cr			ld		
l			dr			lk		
m			fr			pt		
n			gr			xt		
o			pr			mp		
p			tr			sk		
qu			sp			st		
r			sc			lp		
s			sk			sp		
t			sm			nd		
u			sn			lt		
v			sw			lm		
w			tw			nk		

Date started: _____   Date completed: _____

Phonic Spell Check for Consonant Blends

A non-real word spell check should be given to identify the consonant blends the student knows. The words that follow can be photocopied onto cardstock to make word cards. The check should be given in at least two parts: first the initial blends and then the final blends. Mark the blends known on the Phonic Checklist (page 55). Sound cards can be made of those blends not mastered. (See Appendix 6.)

Initial Blends

swul	prip	twil	smoc	slat
snex	triv	flig	grop	frat
crit	dreb	brug	scun	glib
thap	shum	sked	tham	spup
chan	skib	pleb	blag	clem

Final Blends

gesh	folm	dask	reft	zeng
pumb	zock	palt	himp	tross
lasm	upt	gilf	wend	tuxt
murf	hulp	pelk	ront	lusp
yown	vank	zast	vald	tict

Sound Cards

To become accurate readers and spellers, students generally need to know the sound each letter or letter blend represents. Each letter has a shape (symbol) that represents a particular sound. Sound cards can be used to teach students sound-symbol correspondence and should be practiced every day until sound-symbol correspondences are known.

The words that follow can be photocopied onto cardstock and cut into sound cards. If the students cannot read the words then a picture clue can be drawn to represent each word.

The student holds the cards, then does the following:

1. says the word on the card (a picture may be needed as a clue to the word)

   For example:

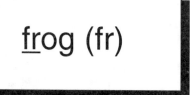

2. listens for the sound of the letters that are underlined

3. says the sound the underlined letters make (the phonetic sound of these letters is given in brackets).

Model this procedure so the students know what is asked of them.

To check that the students can recognize the sound that a symbol represents (grapheme to phoneme) it is useful to write the letter being practiced on the back of each sound card. Ask the student to read the letter side of the sound cards only and to say the sound of the letter.

For example:

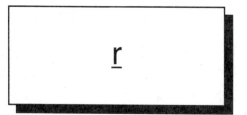

Sound Cards *(cont.)*

To check that the student knows sound-symbol correspondence (phoneme to grapheme):

1. Read the word on each sound card and isolate the sound of the underlined letters.

2. Ask the student to write down the symbols that represent each sound.

3. Check that the symbols are correct for each sound.

Keep a check on progress by recording all of the sound-symbol correspondences the students have learned on the Phonic Checklist (see Appendix 4).

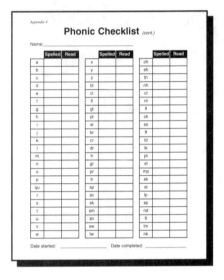

Up to ten sound cards may be given each week, depending on the student's ability. As each sound card is learned, another sound card can be included to make up the number.

Students may know many of the sounds. To check which they know, either the non-real word check can be given (see Appendix 5) or follow this procedure:

1. Read through the sound cards once with the student.

2. Ensure that the student cannot see the cards, then ask him or her to write down the symbols that represent each sound.

3. Record all sound-symbol correspondence known on the Phonic Checklist.

(The sound cards can be photocopied onto cards. It is useful to edge the cards that represent the vowels with a color to make them stand out from the consonants and blends.)

Sound Cards for Single Consonants and Vowel Sounds

apple (a)	egg (e)	Indian (i)
orange (o)	umbrella (u)	bat (b)
cat (k)	dog (d)	fish (f)
goat (g)	house (h)	jacket (j)
kite (k)	lemon (l)	mouse (m)
neck (n)	peg (p)	zebra (z)
rabbit (r)	socks (s)	table (t)
van (v)	window (w)	yellow (y)

Sound Cards for Consonant Blends at the Beginning of Words

thumb (th)	queen (kw)	black (bl)
clown (kl)	flag (fl)	frame (fr)
glove (gl)	plant (pl)	slide (sl)
brown (br)	crab (kr)	drum (dr)
frog (fr)	grapes (gr)	prop (pr)
train (tr)	scarf (sk)	smoke (sm)
snake (sn)	sweets (sw)	twins (tw)
skirt (sk)	spider (sp)	steps (st)

Sound Cards Containing Initial and Final Consonant Blends

bo<u>x</u> (ks)	<u>ch</u>ips (ch)	<u>sh</u>op (sh)
de<u>sk</u> (sk)	mat<u>ch</u> (ch)	ne<u>st</u> (st)
wa<u>sh</u> (sh)	be<u>lt</u> (lt)	mi<u>lk</u> (lk)
a<u>ct</u> (kt)	le<u>ft</u> (ft)	te<u>nt</u> (nt)
ha<u>nd</u> (nd)	si<u>nk</u> (nk)	la<u>mp</u> (mp)
clo<u>ck</u> (k)	ri<u>ng</u> (ng)	<u>spl</u>inter (spl)
<u>spr</u>ing (spr)	<u>str</u>ing (str)	<u>scr</u>ipt (skr)
<u>shr</u>ink (shr)	<u>thr</u>ee (thr)	<u>squ</u>id (skw)

Cards for Word Games

As the *Building Basic Literacy Skills* is phonic-based, students should, in addition, have practice reading the words as whole words.

The pages that follow can be enlarged and photocopied onto cards to make word cards for games that supplement the work of each unit. Playing games is challenging, involves unconscious learning, and is enjoyed by the students. Students can also make their own word cards to take home and reinforce the work learned in class.

One set of each reading card can be used for:

- reading through at speed.

- sorting the cards into families. The students identify the families.

Also, the cards can be used for the following card games:

⇒ **Grab!**

The tutor holds a card up for two seconds only. The players have to write the word down correctly. One point is given for each correct spelling.

⇒ **Matching Families**

The family might be:

- matching a singular word with its plural (e.g., *cat* with *cats*)

- matching a base word with two different endings (e.g., *bat*, *batted*, and *batting*)

In both Matching Families games, five or seven cards are dealt out to each player and the extra cards placed in the center of the table. The top card is turned face up from this pack and placed alongside the pack that is face down to start a second pack of cards.

The first player selects the upturned card if it matches his or her "hand." If not, the player selects a card from the pack that is face down. He or she drops an unwanted card and places it face up on the pile. Players must always have the original number of cards in their hand except for the winning card. The first player to find a matching family wins the game.

Cards for Word Games *(cont.)*

⇒ **Robbers**

A number of cards are placed face up on the table by the dealer. The cards are read by the player. The dealer removes one card while the player is not looking. How many cards can the player remember?

⇒ **Spelling Dice**

The speller throws the dice. The reader counts the number of cards out onto the table, except for the card indicated by the dice number—this is read out to the speller. The speller has to spell the word correctly, and keeps the card if he or she is correct. If he or she spells it incorrectly, then the reader returns the card to the pile. They swap over, and the speller becomes the reader. The student with the most cards at the end of the game wins.

Two of the same cards can be copied and used for:

⇒ **Snap**

To play this game, shuffle the word cards. Deal out all the cards one at a time to each player. Each player keeps his or her cards face down in front of them in a pile. Each time the player's turn comes up, the player turns a card from his or her pile face up, reads the word, and forms a new pile in front of the others.

When two cards of the same word are turned up and read, the first player who has either card and calls "Snap" wins the matched pair. The winner places the cards won under his or her main face-down pile.

If both players call "Snap" at the same time both cards are placed into a pile in the middle of the table. The next player who turns up a card matching those in the pile may call "Snap" and win the cards in the pile.

Anyone calling "Snap" in error places his or her face up cards in the pool. When a player loses all his or her cards, he or she is out of the game. The player who ends up with all the cards wins the game.

⇒ **Concentration**

Place the cards face down on the table. Players alternate turning over two cards. The cards must be read aloud. The object of the game is to find like or corresponding pairs. A player finding a pair can have another go. This game develops the students' concentration and memory.

Unit 1 Cards: Two Syllable Words

suppose	invite	include
confuse	compose	excuse
translate	escape	incline
concave	obtuse	pollute
athlete	membrane	describe
refuse	capsule	despite
intrude	invade	enclose
immune	compute	complete

66

Unit 2 Cards: Two Vowels Together

see	fee	flee
day	tray	say
aid	wait	trail
soak	croak	loaf
beak	pleat	team
feet	greed	bleach
pray	slay	brain
sprain	hoax	stout

Unit 3 Cards: Words that Have Open Syllables

begin	began	remote
refine	omit	direct
focus	oval	silent
final	select	prepare
equip	predict	minus
define	result	rotate
reduce	data	cubic
minor	stamen	modal

Unit 4 Cards: VC/V Words

atom	robot	model
proper	topic	tropic
copy	solid	volume
project	pivot	finish
visit	level	static
planet	profit	adapt
present	vanish	petal
promise	divide	clever

Unit 5 Cards: Vowel + "r" Words

anger	perfect	sister
modern	prefer	carpet
darling	farmer	barber
remark	thirty	birth
skirt	first	flirt
corner	escort	formal
afford	fortune	burn
return	burst	hurt

Answer Key

The *Building Basic Literacy Skills* series is largely self-checking and typical answers for each page of instruction are located in the answer key along with direct points of guidance for the tutor.

Since the students are actively encouraged to take control of their own learning, it may be sensible for the tutor to allow them to mark and rate their own work. This may be monitored by encouraging students to exchange papers to mark a partner's work. This will again involve reading and following instructions, and in itself may encourage the students to think more carefully about the patterns of letters within words.

Answer Key *(cont.)*

Page 12

Combining Syllables

1. Read each syllable then combine them to make words.

		Copy the word.	Look/say/listen/cover/write/check.
com	plete	complete	complete
col	lide	collide	collide
in	clude	include	include
des	cribe	describe	describe

2. Match the syllables to make a real word.

		Write the word.	Look/say/listen/cover/write/check.
a. es	flate	escape	escape
mis	treme	mistake	mistake
in	cape	inflate	inflate
ex	take	extreme	extreme

b. com	lete	complete	complete
ath	plete	athlete	athlete
in	tume	invite	invite
cos	vite	costume	costume

c. ex	close	expose	expose
en	cribe	enclose	enclose
con	pose	concrete	concrete
des	crete	describe	describe

3. Make sure you know what all these words mean. Use a dictionary, if needed.

Page 13

Dividing Syllables

1. Divide these words into syllables (beats). (Remember: find the vowels first, mark the consonants between the vowels, then split the word into two beats.)

vc/cv	1st Beat	2nd Beat	Write the Whole Word
mistake	mis	take	mistake
describe	des	cribe	describe
explode	ex	plode	explode
combine	com	bine	combine
excuse	ex	cuse	excuse
suppose	sup	pose	suppose
inflate	in	flate	inflate
enclose	en	close	enclose
include	in	clude	include

2. Use the words above to complete these sentences.

a. I _____suppose_____ it's my turn to make tea again.

b. The red balloon was about to _____inflate_____ with the hot air.

c. _____Excuse_____ me, I was here before you!

d. If you _____combine_____ peanut butter and chocolate, it tastes good.

e. The bomb was about to _____explode_____.

f. Please _____enclose_____ a stamped addressed envelope.

g. The man had to _____describe_____ his stolen car to the policeman.

h. I would like you to _____include_____ me in your plans to go out.

i. Why do I always make a _____mistake_____ with my spelling?

Page 14

Endings that Begin with a Vowel

1. Add *ed* or *ing* to the silent *e* words. (Remember to take off the silent *e* first, if necessary.) Then complete the sentences so they make sense.

a. I was being chase __d__ by _____so I _____.

b. The bus will be arriv __ing__ at _____ if I do not _____I shall miss it.

c. My red dress fade __d__. Now my socks are _____.

d. She blame __d__ me for _____ when I _____.

e. She was refus __ing__ to _____ so I _____.

2. Underline, then correct, the two spelling mistakes in each sentence. Then add two sentences to finish the story.

I am <u>saveing</u> up to buy some <u>skats</u>. I am <u>hopping</u> one day to be a <u>skateing</u> star. I would be <u>licked</u> by all my <u>fanns</u>. They would yell for me when <u>iam</u> <u>ussing</u> my skates. I cannot wait to be <u>speedeing</u> around the ice like an <u>athleete</u>. I will get the <u>bigest</u> <u>priz</u> on earth! My mom <u>hops</u> I will get married and have children but I _____

Page 15

Endings that Begin with a Consonant

> **i** Do not take off the silent *e* if the suffix (ending) begins with a consonant.

1. The blends *ment*, *ful*, and *less* are suffixes. Choose one of these endings to add to each base word so it makes sense.

use <u>ful</u>	base <u>ment</u>	state <u>ment</u>
grate <u>ful</u>	hope <u>ful</u>	life <u>less</u>
pave <u>ment</u>	waste <u>ful</u>	home <u>less</u>
use <u>less</u>	blame <u>less</u>	hope <u>less</u>

2. Delete the words not needed in the following sentences.

a. The gravy was ~~taste tasting~~ **tasteless**.

b. The man was ~~hoped~~ **hopeful** ~~hopeless~~ he would win the race.

c. I am ~~blame~~ **blameless** ~~blamed~~. It was Tim who broke the jug.

d. That was a silly ~~state~~ **statement** ~~stating~~ you have just made!

3. Choose two of these suffixes—*er*, *less*, *ing*, and *est*—to add to each base word so it makes sense. Write the two new words.

safe	safer	safest
smoke	smoker	smoking
take	taker	taking
ripe	riper	ripest
late	later	latest
explore	explorer	exploring
intrude	intruder	intruding

Answer Key *(cont.)*

Page 16

Unit 1: Two-Syllable Words

Silent "e" Poetry

Read the words in the box. Then use them to complete each line of the poems.

1. | tasteful — plateful — ungrateful — wasteful |

   I think you're so ___ungrateful___

   Not to eat this tasty ___plateful___ .

   It is just so ___wasteful___

   When this dinner is so ___tasteful___ .

2. | impede — inflate — stampede — state |

   Everyone was in a ___state___

   The balloon was about to over- ___inflate___ .

   The balloon grew so big it did ___impede___

   On the people—so they started a ___stampede___ .

3. | intrude — dictate — crude — escape |

   Teachers confuse me, so I try to ___escape___

   When they find me, they make me ___dictate___ .

   I try to ignore them but they always ___intrude___

   "You write this down and stop being ___crude___ ."

Page 17

Unit 1: Two-Syllable Words

Unit 1 Word List

Say the sound of the underlined letters, then read the words. Read across the page from left to right. How many words can you read in one minute?

concrete	invite	suppose	include
confuse	impede	compose	trombone
capsule	excuse	implore	supreme
cascade	translate	empire	escape
incline	oppose	intrude	stampede
concave	obtuse	compose	pollute
explore	costume	inflate	extreme
collide	ignore	immune	inhale
inquire	explode	enclose	describe
dictate	postpone	enzyme	capsule
upgrade	nickname	update	advise
despite	incline	subside	subscribe
compute	exclude	consume	mundane
described	safest	chased	ignored
refused	arrived	latest	inhaler

Which word from the list above means "to ask"? ___inquire___

Page 18

Unit 2: Two Vowels Together

Two Vowels in One Syllable

ℹ️ Reminder: When two vowels go out walking in one syllable, the first one does the talking and says its name. The second vowel says nothing.

1. Say the sound of the underlined vowels then read the word.

see	toe	soap	day	sail
tie	blue	keep	load	cream
mail	east	stay	glue	boat
beak	geese	clay	drain	cue
float	chain	screen	sway	oath
die	scream	cheer	reach	throat

2. Use the words above to complete the sentences.

   a. I nearly choked when the toast stuck in my ___throat___ .

   b. The ___sail___ on the boat was flapping in the wind.

   c. Dad put sugar and ___cream___ in his coffee.

   d. The postman collects the ___mail___ every day but Sunday.

   e. I put the spider on her hair and waited for the ___scream___ .

   f. I stubbed my ___toe___ on the brick near the gate.

   g. The gum stuck like ___glue___ on my dress.

   h. She washed her hands with ___soap___ and water.

   i. The sun rises in the ___east___ .

   j. The ___chain___ on my bike had jammed.

Page 19

Unit 2: Two Vowels Together

Adding Endings

1. Study the words below then fill in the blanks with the correct word.

bead	beads	beaded	beading
stain	stains	stained	staining
greet	greets	greeted	greeting
cheer	cheers	cheered	cheering
load	loads	loaded	loading
float	floats	floated	floating
stay	stays	stayed	staying
cheat	cheats	cheated	cheating
heat	heats	heated	heating

2. Add *s*, *ing*, or *ed* to one word so each sentence makes sense. Write the new sentence on the line provided.

   a. The cat was creep along the wall.
      The cat was creeping along the wall.

   b. Tom need to mend his bike.
      Tom needs to mend his bike.

   c. My mom always greet me with a kiss. Ugh!
      My mom always greets me with a kiss. Ugh!

   d. My dad was speed in his car.
      My dad was speeding in his car.

   e. The two sleeve were rolled up on his shirt.
      The two sleeves were rolled up on his shirt.

   f. The song finished and everyone cheer.
      The song finished and everyone cheered.

   g. I think you cheat on your exam.
      I think you cheated on your exam.

   h. The boat were lined up in the dock.
      The boats were lined up in the dock.

Answer Key *(cont.)*

Page 20

Two Vowel Words

1. Write four words that rhyme with the following words.

treat	boat	creep	raid
beat	coat	steep	braid
heat	goat	sleep	laid
meat	note	sheep	maid
seat	wrote	weep	paid

2. Fill in the missing vowels to complete the following words. Use *ee, oa,* and *ai.* Make sure that no two words are the same.

gr __ee__ n
s __ee__ d
b __ee__ t
s __ee__ k
r __ai__ d
s __ee__ p

gr __oa__ n
s __ai__ d
b __oa__ t
s __oa__ k
r __oa__ d
s __oa__ p

3. Cross out the word or words that are not needed in each of the following sentences.

   a. The toad began to ~~creak~~ croak as he jumped into the moat.

   b. It was a ~~treit~~ treat to shop on Fleet Street.

   c. The bandit went to raid ~~read~~ the comic book store.

   d. Do not ~~mean~~ moan about your homework.

   e. The ~~bread~~ braid in her hair is ~~grain~~ green.

   f. The cake had grated orange ~~pail~~ peel in it, and it got stuck in my teeth.

Page 21

Edit and Revise

1. Add *ing* or *ed* to words in each sentence of the story so it makes sense. Complete the story in your own words.

> Her finger was bleed^{ing} so I put a bandage on it. She was scream^{ing} so much she said she felt like faint^{ing}. As she spoke she keel^{ed} over and landed in an open drain at the side of the path. She was now soak^{ing} wet and she smell^{ed} horribly. She began screech^{ing}. I thought she had been maim^{ed} for life but she had only _____
>
> _____
>
> _____.

2. Match the words in present tense to those in past tense. Then use each word to complete the sentences below.

Present tense	Past tense
lay	laid
say	said
pay	paid

   a. I ___lay___ my keys on the table when I get home from school.

   b. Yesterday, I ___laid___ two quarters on my desk. Now I can't find them!

   c. I ___paid___ 70 cents to buy two candy bars at school the other day.

   d. Tomorrow, I will ___pay___ 75 cents to ride the bus.

   e. If they ask me to go, I will ___say___, "No, thank you!"

   f. He ___said___ I had to give him his book back.

Page 22

Two-Vowel Poetry

Read the words then use them to complete each line of the poems.

1. | float — moat — boat — throat |

   Did **you** know that **I** can ___float___?

   So **I** don't need to buy a ___boat___.

   I'll jump straight in and **sw**im t**he** ___moat___

   I hope **I** don't get a frog stuck in my ___throat___.

2. | train — chain — drain — rain |

   I was standing in the ___rain___

   Just waiting for the 11:00 ___train___

   Whe**n I** lost my silver ___chain___.

   It just went down the ___drain___!

3. | scream — cream — weasels — measels |

   Di**d y**ou know that the ___measels___

   Is a disease that attacks ___weasels___?

   If you're squeamish, please don't ___scream___

   But they eat dead frogs covered in ___cream___.

Page 23

Unit 2 Word List

 Say the underlined vowel sounds then read the words. Read across the page from left to right. How many words can you read in one minute?

s<u>ee</u>	<u>ai</u>d	t<u>ea</u>	d<u>ay</u>
<u>oa</u>t	f<u>ee</u>	f<u>ai</u>l	b<u>ea</u>k
pl<u>ay</u>	g<u>oa</u>t	ch<u>ea</u>p	h<u>ai</u>l
fr<u>ea</u>k	tr<u>ay</u>	cl<u>oa</u>k	bl<u>ee</u>d
f<u>ai</u>nt	bl<u>ea</u>ch	sw<u>ay</u>	thr<u>oa</u>t
wh<u>ee</u>ze	r<u>ai</u>se	pl<u>ea</u>d	sl<u>ay</u>
sh<u>ee</u>t	br<u>ai</u>n	dr<u>ea</u>m	pr<u>ay</u>
t<u>oa</u>st	bl<u>ee</u>d	pr<u>ai</u>se	pl<u>ea</u>t
cl<u>ay</u>	b<u>oa</u>st	sw<u>ee</u>t	gl<u>ea</u>m
p<u>ay</u>	s<u>oa</u>k	b<u>ee</u>ch	b<u>ea</u>ch
bl<u>ea</u>ch	l<u>oa</u>f	l<u>ea</u>f	cr<u>oa</u>k
b<u>oa</u>t	k<u>ee</u>n	g<u>ee</u>se	t<u>ea</u>m
s<u>ee</u>m	s<u>ea</u>m	tw<u>ee</u>d	scr<u>ee</u>n
fr<u>ee</u>ze	spr<u>ai</u>n	f<u>ai</u>th	p<u>ai</u>nt
h<u>ea</u>ve	<u>oa</u>k	sn<u>ai</u>l	tr<u>ai</u>l

There are five different vowel patterns in the list above. Name them.

___ee___ ___ai___ ___ea___ ___ay___ ___oa___

Answer Key (cont.)

Page 24

Unit 3: Syllables Ending with a Vowel

The V/CV Pattern

> **i** Some two-syllable words only have one consonant between the vowels so the word is split before the consonant:
>
> music — mu / sic
>
> The vowel of the first syllable is open, so it says its name.

1. These words have been split for you. Read each syllable and listen for the word. Then look, say, listen, cover, write, and check!

be	gin	begin	bo	nus	bonus
mu	sic	music	hu	man	human
la	dy	lady	fi	nal	final
o	ver	over	ze	ro	zero

2. Now find the syllables of the following words. Mark the vowels, and then divide the words into syllables using the v/cv pattern.

vc/cv	1st Syllable	2nd Syllable	Write the Whole Word
moment	mo	ment	moment
chosen	cho	sen	chosen
minus	mi	nus	minus
taken	ta	ken	taken
remote	re	mote	remote
gravy	gra	vy	gravy
item	i	tem	item
Friday	Fri	day	Friday

3. Read the words again.

Page 25

Unit 3: Syllables Ending with a Vowel

Matching Syllables

1. Read the syllables and match them up to make a word. Then look, say, listen, cover, write, and check!

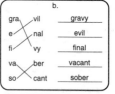

a.
- o — over
- di — direct
- mu — music
- Ju — July
- hu — human

b.
- gra — gravy
- e — evil
- fi — final
- va — vacant
- so — sober

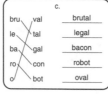

c.
- bru — brutal
- le — legal
- ba — bacon
- ro — robot
- o — oval

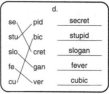

d.
- se — secret
- stu — stupid
- slo — slogan
- fe — fever
- cu — cubic

2. Choose from the words above to complete each sentence.

a. I ate _____ bacon _____ and eggs for breakfast.

b. I like _____ gravy _____ on my mashed potatoes.

c. A robot is not a _____ human _____ being.

d. You must always keep a _____ secret _____.

e. I will _____ direct _____ you onto the right path.

f. If you feel hot and ill, you may have a _____ fever _____.

g. The U.S. president's office has an _____ oval _____ shape.

h. I like pop _____ music _____ better than rap.

Page 26

Unit 3: Syllables Ending with a Vowel

Words Ending in "al"

1. Add the letters *al* to complete the second syllable. Combine the syllables to find the word. Then look, say, listen, cover, write, and check!

fin	al	final	loc	al	local
equ	al	equal	brut	al	brutal
leg	al	legal	riv	al	rival
tot	al	total	spin	al	spinal

2. Complete the sentences using the words above.

a. The _____ local _____ news and weather forecast can be found on TV.

b. The shopping bill came to a _____ total _____ of $88.76.

c. To make a cake, you need _____ equal _____ amounts of sugar and flour.

d. Carl has a _____ rival _____ who is interested in his girlfriend.

e. The _____ brutal _____ man kicked the dog out of his way.

f. Fortunately, he didn't damage his _____ spinal _____ cord in the accident.

g. The _____ final _____ lap of the race will be worth watching.

3. Look at the words below. Then complete the blanks by following the pattern.

final	finals	finally
equal	equals	equally
local	locals	locally
total	totals	totally

4. Now read the words.

Page 27

Unit 3: Syllables Ending with a Vowel

Types of Syllables

> **i** **Open syllables** end in one vowel. The vowel says its name.
> **Closed-in syllables** have one vowel and end in a consonant. The vowel says its short sound.
> **r** **Silent *e* syllables** have one vowel followed by one consonant, followed by *e*. The vowel says its name.

1. Underline the vowels in the following words. Look at the syllables. Decide which sort of syllable they are, and then write each syllable under the correct heading below. The first syllables has been placed for you.

fa – tal	re – tire	ar – rive	re – late	in – trude
pri – vate	si – lent	e – ven	stu – pid	com – plete

Ends with a Vowel: Open Syllable	Vowel Closed In by a Consonant: Closed-in Syllable	Last Syllable of the Word, Ends in *e*: Silent *e* Syllable
fa	tal	tire
re	ar	rive
pri	in	late
si	lent	trude
e	ven	vate
stu	pid	plete
	com	

2. Use a word from above to complete each sentence.

a. The child did not say anything. He was _____ silent _____.

b. Two is an _____ even _____ number.

c. I wish to _____ retire _____ from work at sixty years of age.

d. Do not _____ arrive _____ late for the funeral service.

e. Please _____ complete _____ your work and then hand it in to me.

Answer Key *(cont.)*

Page 28

Unit 3: Syllables Ending with a Vowel

Syllables Ending with a Vowel Poetry

Read the words then use them to complete each line of the poems.

1. | insect — object — protect — dissect |

In science class, we had to _____ dissect _____

A little tiny blue and black _____ insect _____.

I felt so bad; I wanted to _____ protect _____

That poor little thing. I had to _____ object _____.

2. | decline — cosine — define — Caroline |

In English class, we had to _____ define _____

The mathematical term _____ cosine _____.

But a stubborn girl named _____ Caroline _____

Shook her head and said, "I _____ decline _____."

3. | over — Rover — crazy — lazy |

Why are you so _____ lazy _____?

You must be completely _____ crazy _____.

Your exams will soon be _____ over _____

Then you can nap with your dog, _____ Rover _____.

Page 29

Unit 3: Syllables Ending with a Vowel

Unit 3 Word List

Read the underlined syllables then practice reading and spelling the words. (The first syllable is an open syllable and so the vowel will say its name.) How many words can you read in one minute?

begin	began	remote	refine
demon	omit	direct	cupid
stupid	music	focus	bonus
human	tulip	cubic	July
widen	oval	even	gravy
evil	Venus	vocal	rival
index	lazy	crazy	zero
taken	basic	item	able
desire	label	direct	silent
final	defy	slogan	prepare
open	pilot	solo	select
equip	equate	over	delete
severe	deplete	begun	reduce
deflate	primate	became	fatal
hotel	pupil	humid	unit

Which of the words above means "to use up or exhaust"? _____ deplete _____

Page 30

Unit 4: VC/V Words

"Robin Words"

 When one consonant or consonant blend is between two vowels, try v/cv first. However, look at these words: *robin, prison, method, limit*. If we put the slash (/) after the vowel, it would make the vowel say its name! In these words, divide after the consonant vc/v. This will make the vowel say its short sound because the vowel is "closed in." Examples: *rob/in, pris/on, meth/od, lim/it*

1. Combine the syllables to make a real word. Then look, say, listen, cover, write, and check!

gren	ade	grenade	sev	en	seven
val	id	valid	sol	id	solid
riv	er	river	lim	it	limit
men	nu	menu	lem	on	lemon
pris	on	prison	pan	ic	panic

2. Choose one of the words to complete each sentence.

a. There are _____ seven _____ days in a week.

b. The warranty was not _____ valid _____ because it was out of date.

c. When the robbers entered the bank, we all began to _____ panic _____

d. The ducks were swimming down the _____ river _____.

e. People who do wrong are locked up in _____ prison _____.

f. I _____ limit _____ myself to three chips; otherwise I would eat them all.

g. There are three states of matter: _____ solid _____, liquid, and gas.

h. Our school _____ menu _____ includes a salad with everything.

i. The soldier took out the hand- _____ grenade _____ and hurled it at the tank.

Page 31

Unit 4: VC/V Words

Dividing VC/V Syllables

1. Divide the following words into two syllables, using vc/v.

vc/cv	1st Syllable	2nd Syllable	Cover and Write the Word
polish	pol	ish	polish
travel	trav	el	travel
lemon	lem	on	lemon
ever	ev	er	ever
clever	clev	er	clever
solid	sol	id	solid
vanish	van	ish	vanish
never	nev	er	never
comic	com	ic	comic

2. Read the following. Then match the syllables to make a real word.

a.

met	im	metal
den	en	denim
fin	al	finish
clev	ish	clever
lin	er	linen

b.

cred	apt	credit
ad	en	adapt
tal	it	talent
lem	ent	lemon
sev	on	seven

c.

riv	ic	river
pan	ish	panic
mel	el	melon
rad	er	radish
grav	on	gravel

d.

hab	il	habit
ev	en	evil
sliv	it	sliver
men	er	menu
giv	u	given

Answer Key *(cont.)*

Page 32

Verb Sense

Add *ing* and *ed* to the verb. Then use one of the words to complete each sentence. The first one has been done for you.

1. polish ___polished___ ___polishing___

   The man was ___polishing___ the table top.

   The man ___polished___ the table top.

2. finish ___finished___ ___finishing___

   I was just ___finishing___ my dinner when there was a knock on the front door.

   I had just ___finished___ my dinner when there was a knock on the front door.

3. adapt ___adapted___ ___adapting___

   The TV man ___adapted___ the channels to pick up satellite TV.

   The TV man was ___adapting___ the channels to pick up satellite TV.

4. promise ___promised___ ___promising___

   My dad ___promised___ to buy me a bike for my birthday.

   My dad was ___promising___ to buy me a bike for my birthday.

5. travel ___traveled___ ___traveling___

   The bus was ___traveling___ at 30 miles per hour through the shopping center.

   The bus ___traveled___ at 30 miles per hour through the shopping center.

Page 33

Words Ending with "ic" and "ish"

> i | Words with more than one syllable that end with the sound /ik/ are spelled *ic*.

1. Add *ic* or *ish* to the syllables below to make a real word. Then look, say, listen, cover, write, and check!

   clin _ic_   clinic   com _ic_   comic

   van _ish_   vanish   pun _ish_   punish

   frol _ic_   frolic   rad _ish_   radish

   stat _ic_   static   mim _ic_   mimic

   fin _ish_   finish   pol _ish_   polish

   trop _ic_   tropic   ep _ic_   epic

2. Match these meanings to the words above. The first has been done for you.

   a. kids' magazine — comic

   b. red vegetable — radish

   c. disappear — vanish

   d. not moving — static

   e. end — finish

   f. copy someone's voice — mimic

   g. cause pain to someone — punish

   h. just north or south of the equator — tropic

   i. have fun — frolic

   j. to make clean and shiny — polish

   k. very long book or film — epic

   l. place to get medical help — clinic

Page 34

Using "Robin Words"

1. Choose the best word to complete the sentence. Then cross out the others. Be careful to look for the base words.

   a. The man was ~~polish~~ polished ~~polishing~~ the windows.

   b. Ms. Gill will ~~travel~~ ~~travels~~ traveling around the world next year.

   c. Jenny is ~~study~~ studying at Blackburn College this year.

   d. Odd socks seem to be ~~vanish~~ ~~vanished~~ vanishing after every wash.

   e. The room was ~~panel~~ ~~panels~~ paneled in oak. It looked very grand.

   f. I shall be ~~visit~~ ~~visited~~ visiting my family at Christmas.

2. Underline the "robin words" as you read the story. Complete the story using your own words.

   The <u>tenor</u> was singing so high that a <u>button</u> shot from his <u>cravat</u> and landed on a <u>radish</u> on someone's plate of <u>salad</u>. His face went red and <u>shriveled</u>. It was <u>comical</u>. I wasn't the only one who started laughing. I couldn't help it. The man <u>finished</u> his <u>tribute</u> to Elvis and then <u>vanished</u> from the stage.

   I just _____

   _____

   _____

3. Write the "robin words" on the lines below.

   tenor   salad   finished

   button   shriveled   tribute

   cravat   comical   vanished

   radish

Page 35

"Robin Words" Poetry

1. | ever — muddy — clever — study |

   I work hard to be ___clever___.

   I read forever and ___ever___.

   But I found that too much ___study___

   Makes my poor brain ___muddy___.

2. | camel — travel — gravel — mammal |

   Would you like to ride on a ___camel___?

   With a hump, it's quite an odd ___mammal___.

   They'll cross sand or dirt or ___gravel___.

   Sometimes, it's the best way to ___travel___.

3. | rivet — pivot — attic — static |

   There was a man who went to the ___attic___.

   He saw a ghost; his hair went ___static___.

   He ran downstairs and then did a ___pivot___.

   He nailed the door with a steel ___rivet___.

Answer Key *(cont.)*

Page 36

Unit 4: VC/V Words

Unit 4 Word List

> Read the underlined syllable then practice reading and spelling the words. (Remember to read across the page from left to right.) How many words can you read in one minute?

atom	comet	tenor	menu
lily	livid	robin	model
proper	topic	tropic	copy
comic	polish	body	solid
volume	project	novel	modern
product	study	punish	river
widow	linen	mimic	sliver
pivot	venom	method	visit
prison	finish	tribute	seven
metal	denim	tepid	melon
credit	(never)	present	(clever)
lemon	pedal	level	planet
rigid	model	grenade	valid
talent	camel	panel	gravel
magic	radish	static	profit

1. Circle the words that rhyme with *ever*. How many are there? ____2____

Page 37

Unit 5: Vowels Followed by "r"

Charting "r" Words

> **i** When *r* follows one vowel, together they make one sound.
> • *er* ➡ hammer (sound: /ur/)
> • *ir* ➡ bird: (sound: /ur/)
> • *ur* ➡ church: (sound: /ur/)
> • *ar* ➡ cart: (sound: /ar/)
> • *or* ➡ fork: (sound: /or/)

Underline the vowels that have *r* after them. Then look, say, listen, cover, write, and check, putting the words into the correct list.

church	card	her	smart	bird	hurt
cork	turn	term	thorn	burn	skirt
form	bark	north	fern	born	dart
mark	herb	sharp	herd	short	birth
third	flirt	churn	perm	burst	first

er	ir	ur	or	ar
her	bird	church	cork	card
term	skirt	hurt	thorn	smart
fern	birth	turn	form	bark
herb	third	burn	north	dart
herd	flirt	churn	born	mark
perm	first	burst	short	sharp

Page 38

Unit 5: Vowels Followed by "r"

Matching "r" Syllables

1. Match the syllables to make a real word. Then look, say, listen, cover, write, and check!

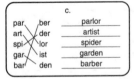

a.
but	ver	butter
whis	der	whisper
an	ter	anger
thun	ger	thunder
sil	per	silver

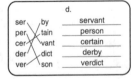

b.
bet	ner	better
tem	mer	temper
ham	per	hammer
num	ter	number
din	ber	dinner

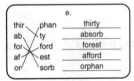

c.
par	ber	parlor
art	der	artist
spi	lor	spider
gar	ist	garden
bar	den	barber

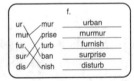

d.
ser	by	servant
per	tain	person
cer	vant	certain
der	dict	derby
ver	son	verdict

e.
thir	phan	thirty
ab	ty	absorb
for	ford	forest
af	est	afford
or	sorb	orphan

f.
ur	mur	urban
mur	prise	murmur
fur	turb	furnish
sur	ban	surprise
dis	nish	disturb

2. Look back and check your spellings. Check to be sure that you know what each word means.

Page 39

Unit 5: Vowels Followed by "r"

Dividing "r" Syllables

1. Keeping *ir*, *er*, *ur*, *or*, and *ar* together, divide the following words into two syllables using vc/cv or v/cv patterns.

vc/cv	1st Syllable	2nd Syllable	Write the Whole Word
dirty	dir	ty	dirty
perfect	per	fect	perfect
formal	for	mal	formal
curtsy	curt	sy	curtsy
darling	dar	ling	darling
thirty	thir	ty	thirty
absorb	ab	sorb	absorb
turnip	tur	nip	turnip
expert	ex	pert	expert
remark	re	mark	remark
sober	so	ber	sober

2. Use the words above to complete these sentences.

a. My dad ate a carrot and a ____turnip____.

b. My aunt turns ____thirty____ on her next birthday.

c. Girls sometimes ____curtsy____ after the final act of a show.

d. I do not know anyone who is ____perfect____.

e. Paper towels ____absorb____ liquid very quickly.

f. Dress was ____formal____ at the party, so I did not wear my jeans.

g. I am an ____expert____ on my computer.

Answer Key *(cont.)*

Page 40

Unit 5: Vowels Followed by "r"

Rhymes with "ore"

> **i** Words with *ore* rhyme with *sore*.

1. Write out these words with *ore* as their ending sound. Look, say, listen, cover, write, and check!

more	more	core	core	sore	sore
snore	snore	swore	swore	before	before
tore	tore	score	score	implore	implore
ignore	ignore				

2. Use the words above to complete the blanks in the story below.

The football game was very slow. There was no _____score_____, and the man next to me began to _____snore_____. He was asleep! I was surprised to the _____core_____. My throat was _____swore_____ from shouting. When we lost the game, I _____swore_____ I would never go to any _____more_____ football games again. I will _____ignore_____ my friends who _____implore_____ me to support my team. I actually _____tore_____ up my season ticket. _____Before_____ you say anything, it was last year's ticket!

3. Study the words and complete the blanks to fit the pattern.

snore	snored	snoring
score	scored	scoring
ignore	ignored	ignoring

Page 41

Unit 5: Vowels Followed by "r"

Rhymes with "are"

> **i** Words with *are* rhyme with *hair*.

1. Write out these words with *are* as their ending sound. Look, say, listen, cover, write, and check!

bare	bare	square	square	share	share
stare	stare	compare	compare	beware	beware
care	care	glare	glare	scare	scare
fare	fare	declare	declare	prepare	prepare

2. Use the words above to complete the blanks in the sentences below.

a. The ghost in that movie didn't _____scare_____ me.

b. Basic shapes include circle, _____square_____, and triangle.

c. Don't _____stare_____ at the sun during an eclipse.

d. She tried to _____prepare_____ dinner before 6:00.

e. The sign read, "_____Beware_____ of the guard dog."

3. Study the words and complete the blanks to fit the pattern.

declare	declared	declaring
share	shared	sharing
glare	glared	glaring

Page 42

Unit 5: Vowels Followed by "r"

Double "r" Words

> **i** **r** When a word has two *r*'s together, the vowels do not join with the *r*, they say their own sound.

1. Read each syllable then combine them to make words.

		Copy the word	Look/say/listen/cover/write/check
car	ry	carry	carry
hur	ry	hurry	hurry
squir	rel	squirrel	squirrel
ber	ry	berry	berry
ar	rive	arrive	arrive
hor	ror	horror	horror
cher	ry	cherry	cherry
er	ror	error	error

2. Match the syllables to make a real word.

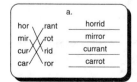

a.
hor	rant	horrid
mir	rot	mirror
cur	rid	currant
car	ror	carrot

b.
ter	rot	terror
quar	rect	quarrel
par	ror	parrot
cor	rel	correct

Page 43

Unit 5: Vowels Followed by "r"

The Letter "r" Poetry

Read the words then use them to complete each line of the poems.

1. **term — letter — better — germ**

I caught this awful _____germ_____

During the last school _____term_____.

My mother wrote the school a _____letter_____

Saying I'd return when I felt _____better_____.

2. **fur — spider — error — terror**

The old lady was filled with _____terror_____

When she realized her _____error_____.

It was not a stain on her coat of _____fur_____

But a big fat hairy _____spider_____.

3. **cherry — garden — pardon — carry**

I said to the farmer, "I beg your _____pardon_____,

But where is the vegetable _____garden_____?

"Look for the sign with a big red _____cherry_____.

You'll find produce—all you can _____carry_____."

Notes

_____

_____

_____

_____

_____

_____

_____

_____

_____

_____

_____

_____